Tomahawk Beckwourth

My Life and Adventures

Adapted by Michael Cox

Illustrated by Barbara Lofthouse

OXFORD
UNIVERSITY PRESS

56408 41

OXFORD
UNIVERSITY PRESS

Great Clarendon Street, Oxford OX2 6DP

Oxford University Press is a department of the University of Oxford.
It furthers the University's objective of excellence in research, scholarship,
and education by publishing worldwide in

Oxford New York

Auckland Cape Town Dar es Salaam Hong Kong Karachi
Kuala Lumpur Madrid Melbourne Mexico City Nairobi
New Delhi Shanghai Taipei Toronto

With offices in

Argentina Austria Brazil Chile Czech Republic France Greece
Guatemala Hungary Italy Japan Poland Portugal Singapore
South Korea Switzerland Thailand Turkey Ukraine Vietnam

Oxford is a registered trade mark of Oxford University Press
in the UK and in certain other countries

British Library Cataloguing in Publication Data

Data available

ISBN-13: 978-0-19-919660-9
ISBN-10: 0-19-919660-5

5 7 9 10 8 6 4

Mixed Pack (1 of 6 different titles): ISBN 0 19 919662 1
Class Pack (6 copies of 6 titles): ISBN 0 19 919661 3

Illustrated by Barbara Lofthouse c/o Artist Partners
Cover photo by C Waldo Love/Colorado Historical Society

Acknowledgements
p1 Eastman Studio Portrait/Plumas County Museum;
p4/5 Corel; p5 Geoffrey Clements/Corbis UK Ltd.;
p7 Hulton|Archive/Getty Images; p16/17 Geoffrey
Clements/Corbis UK Ltd.; p18/19 Hulton|Archive/Getty
Images; p23 Corbis UK Ltd.; p24/25 Joseph Sohm; Visions of
America/Corbis UK Ltd.; p43 Missouri Historical Society, St.
Louis; p51 Mary Evans Picture Library; p55 Bridgeman Art
Library; p60 Bettmann/Corbis UK Ltd.; p61 Bettmann/Corbis
UK Ltd.; p78 Hulton|Archive/Getty Images; p78/79 Corel

Printed in China

Contents

Introduction

When Christopher Columbus discovered America in 1492, people were already living there. These people, now known as Native Americans, had been there for at *least* 15,000 years. Christopher Columbus called them Indians, because he thought America was India (well, we all make mistakes!).

Soon, Europeans rushed to America to claim great chunks of it for themselves. By 1800, all of America's east coast had been settled. They displaced the Native Americans and imported Africans to work as slaves.

After **Independence**, the new USA gained an extra slice of land.

It was a vast, untamed wilderness, home to Indians, grizzly bear, deer, mountain lions and a hundred million buffalo.

From the beginning, the 'Wild West' was explored by all sorts of brave adventurers. One of them was James (Jim) Beckwourth, the son of a white landowner and a black slave. He lived a most incredible life, trapping, blazing trails, living amongst Indians, and leading wagon trains.

By 1890, most of the Indians had been killed or driven from their homes. Of those original hundred million buffalo, only 541 were left!

In 1952 the Americans made a movie about Jim's amazing life. He was played by a *white* actor! This was very much the way of things then. Black Americans were understandably outraged.

The American wilderness

CHAPTER

The Howling Wilderness

I think it must have been around the time I had the fight with Mad Bill Payne that some young fellow asked me to tell him the scariest thing that's ever happened to me. And I couldn't! Why? Because I've had just too many terrifying and hair-raising things happen to me!

Truth is, ever since I was knee-high to a shotgun, I've spent my whole life dodging death and danger. But now it occurs to me that a bullet, arrow, or wild **critter** is gonna get me sooner or later. So, over the next few pages, I'm gonna write down some of my adventures and scrapes. Not all of them though, because that would need a book a hundred times bigger than this one!

My name's James "Tomahawk" Beckwourth and, during the last sixty years or so, I've lived and fought my way through some of the wildest and most thrilling times in America's history. I've battled with Indians, Mexicans, white men and black men.

I've near starved to death, froze to death and near been killed to death with tomahawks and guns. I've blazed trails in the Rocky Mountains, lived as an Indian chief, been a fur-trapper, saloon-keeper, trader, despatch-rider, farmer, horse-thief and army-scout.

I've led wagon trains halfway across America and discovered a route through the mountains to California – the Beckwourth Pass, named after me. And I'm still here to tell the tale.

First off, I'll describe myself, so you've got some sort of picture of me to carry in your head.

I'm what many folk describe as a hardscrabble sort of man.

I dress in fringed buckskin shirts, leggings and moccasins and I stand two metres tall. My black hair is long and at one time it reached past my waist. My skin's black too, but not as black as my hair, and over the years its been scarred by bullets, arrows and war-axes.

My ears are pierced and I wear gold earrings and chains and braid my hair or tie it with ribbons. I'm strong and muscular and I'm a cheerful sort of man who enjoys singing and having a laugh.

As to my skills, they're many: I speak English, French and Spanish – and Indian languages too. I know the Indian ways better than anyone and can track, hunt and scout. I'm expert with dagger, tomahawk and gun and a skilful horseman who knows all manner of tricks. I can ride a galloping horse bareback, then hang upside down so my hair brushes the earth.

Now I'll tell you a bit about my folks. My daddy was Sir Jennings Beckwourth whose family came from England to America, generations back. He was an educated man with noble ancestors going back to the days of the Norman Conquest. My great grand-daddy (times about fifty, I reckon!) helped William whip Harold at the Battle of Hastings in 1066 and was rewarded with a title and lands. Which is why my own Pa was a Sir ... God rest his soul.

My Ma wasn't nearly so high falutin' as my Pa. She was a black slave whose family had been brought to America from Africa to work on the plantations. I don't exactly know how they met, but they got together and had little me.

I was born around about 1800 in Virginia County, which is where I lived with my folks and my twelve brothers and sisters. (Although most of them didn't share the same Ma as me.)

Some time later, we moved to a backwoods settlement near St Louis. It was a howling wilderness of a place surrounded by huge forests, home to hostile Indians and grizzly bear and all manner of other perilous things.

While my Pa and the settlers worked the land, they'd divide themselves into two groups. One would work and one would guard against Indian attacks. They also built a log blockhouse in the centre of our little settlement. At first sign of danger, we'd all rush in there and defend our lives.

Growing up there, us kids soon learned the ways of the woods and how to watch out for ourselves. But I'll never forget the day when I was nine and Pa sent me off to get a sack of flour from a mill some miles away.

On the way back, I called to see my playmates who lived close by. As I rode my horse up to their backyard fence, I saw something that made my blood run cold and tears fill my eyes. Stretched out on the grass before me were the bodies of my little pals and their Ma and Pa. They'd all been murdered by marauding Indians! But what made me really shake from head to toe was when I saw that they had all been scalped!

So this is how I grew up. During this time, my Pa taught me how to behave like a gentleman and to read and write and do numbers. When I grew a bit older and was getting strong, I went to work for a blacksmith in St Louis. Me and him didn't see eye to eye, though. And when I started seeing a very pretty young lady, we got to falling out proper. I was late for work one morning and he yelled at me. So I yelled back. Before I knew it, we were trading blows. I soon got the better of him and had him on his knees. But then a constable arrived, so I had to **skedaddle**, quick sharp.

There was no going back after that. So quite soon, I stole aboard a boat that was bound for Fever River. I'd heard that was where men were mining for lead and there was money to be made.

Fever River was a rough and ready place. Folks lived in huts and tents, perched high on muddy riverbanks. Life was tough. There was typhoid and scurvy everywhere and the settlers spent long, miserable winters hunkered down in the mine shafts for warmth and safety.

There were Indians here, too. They sometimes gave trouble to the miners and settlers, but they didn't bother me. Often, I was out wandering in the woods when I'd come across a band of them cutting up a deer they'd killed, and I'd join them. They soon became my friends and showed me the choicest places for hunting.

After spending some eighteen months at Fever River, I decided to roam further, and caught a steamboat to New Orleans in Louisiana. But then I caught something else ... the yellow fever. This forced me to return to my father's house! But not for long. I was now desperate to be off again, looking for adventure and fame.

CHAPTER

Mountain Man Beckwourth

In the summer of 1824, after my recovery from fever, I heard General William H. Ashley was taking a trapping expedition out west. Suddenly, I wanted more than anything to see the Rocky Mountains and the great Western wilderness I'd heard so much about. So I signed up in a flash!

Now, before I go further in my tale, I must tell you that just before I was born, all of the land that lay between the Mississippi and the Rockies was claimed by the French. But, in 1803, Napoleon Bonaparte sold it to the USA. This more than doubled the size of our country. Only thing was, no one knew **squitty** about our 800,000 square miles of new territory! Or how to find their way around it!

There weren't proper maps, roads or trails. So, back in the 1820s, when I was young and eager for excitement, all of the American West was still a vast unexplored place. It was covered by mountains, forests and thousands of miles of grassy plains, all full of Indians,

eagles, grizzly bear, mountain lions, elk, buffalo, deer and beaver. In other words, an adventurer's paradise! What more could a young, thrill-seeking fellow ask for?

The American West

Moving West around 1865

All sorts of brave and daring men were making their way into the Wild West, seeking fame and fortune. Many drowned in rivers, got lost, starved, froze or perished at the hands of the Indians and the claws of grizzlies and mountain lions. But others, like myself, Jim Bridger, Kit Carson, and Jedediah Smith made our names by blazing new trails. We paved the way for the settlers who later followed us in their thousands, building shanty towns that would soon turn into the great cities of America.

So, in 1824, bursting with excitement, I set off on my first trapping expedition with General Ashley's outfit, the Rocky Mountain Fur Company. I planned to make my fortune from furs whilst gaining fame from the way I handled the tough times that came along. And things did get tough!

We set off, a party of thirty trappers and hunters. We had fifty packhorses, carrying what we thought was enough food and supplies to get us through the winter. How wrong can you be!

Our food was gone in no time. Then the weather turned against us. I'd never known it was possible to be so cold, tired, miserable and hungry. Soon, I was thinking I'd rather be back with that pesky blacksmith than the waist-high snow drifts and howling blizzards that turned us all into living snowmen. Things got so bad that we were forced to kill and eat some of our horses and then we had to become pack animals ourselves.

General Ashley gave orders for the best shots in our party to search for game, so I set

off with my rifle. After a short time I spied a duck, which I then killed. I'm ashamed to say that I ate that duck, giving no thought to my starving friends back in camp.

I felt bad about that and vowed that from that moment on, I would share my last biscuit, my last shilling or my only blanket with a friend in need. And, fortunately, I was able to do just that. Just a few minutes after my terrible selfishness, I spied a large buck and brought it down with one shot.

Then, as I dragged it back to camp, a huge, snarling white wolf came bounding towards me! This I also brought down with a bullet in its brain. Some time later, I also bagged three, good-sized elk. I finally returned to our camp laden with meat and I was greeted as a hero.

However, the cold doubles men's hunger. It wasn't long before our meat was gone. Blizzards turned our flesh blue and our blood to slush, and just when we feared we couldn't last another night, six Indians walked into our camp. With much hand waving, they showed us they wanted us to follow them.

They seemed friendly enough, so we did. Soon we arrived at their tepees where they showed us great kindness, feeding us and looking after our horses for many weeks to come. So, as result of this generous act, we survived the winter.

When spring arrived, we left our Indian friends and began trapping once more.

We now fell in love with the land we had hated throughout the winter. I hardly know

A tepee in winter. A Native American (the name for all people belonging to one of the Indian or Red Indian groups) is carrying a bundle of sticks into her home. When a fire is lit inside, these tent-like constructions can be very warm indeed

how to describe the magical beauty of spring in the Rockies: the wild flowers, shimmering peaks, majestic canyons, gorges filled with tumbling melt water, the brilliant stars in the velvet night sky and the air so clear and sharp you can see a man from a mile away.

After that first spring in the mountains, none of us would ever again be ordinary men. Now, dressed only in the skins of animals we killed, we set about collecting our rich harvest of beaver furs. Then, having gathered all we could carry, we journeyed back east and sold them for a good profit.

The following year, 1825, we set out again. Once more, we went through a hellish winter followed by a perfect spring. This was also the year of the first Mountain Man Rendezvous, an event that would be repeated for years to come. After surviving months of sub-zero temperatures, trapping beaver and fighting off wolves and grizzlies, all of us mountain men would get together. We'd swap tales, drink whiskey, argue about the best and worst places to find furs, occasionally fight, and generally have a good time.

Spring in the mountains

So this was the life I led for the next four years, trapping and exploring, meeting wild animals like eagles, grizzlies, mountain lions, elk, buffalo, deer and beaver, and even wilder men and having all sorts of hair-raising adventures. Like the time me and my **pardners** were making our way through the Snake River valley. We spotted smoke signals rising from the hills above us.

Soon afterwards, we heard loud singing and saw about five hundred mounted Indians galloping towards us. With horror, we recognised them as Blackfeet, famous for their love of scalps!

We raced away. But, as we did, an old man in our party took an arrow in his back and tumbled from his horse. I turned, hoping to rescue him, but six Blackfeet fell on him and scalped him before I could lift a finger!

We now reached a clump of willow trees where we saw a group of about thirty men, women and children crouched in the bushes, screaming in terror at the sight of the Indians.

Realising that we must not let the Blackfeet reach the women and kids, about fifty of my companions and I turned our horses and charged back at the Blackfeet, firing as we did. Soon Indians were crashing from their horses, brought down by our bullets and musket balls.

Clinging to my horse's mane like grim death, I bent low and rode through the Blackfeet lines, wounding some six or seven as I did. I now galloped back down the river valley, knowing two hundred or so trappers •

Half an hour later, I led those trappers in a furious attack on the Indians, and, after a ferocious battle that left dozens of them dead and the rest galloping off in panic, we got through to the trapped women and children who, I am glad to say, were all unharmed!

And then there was the time when a group of my pals and I were sitting outside our tents, chatting and drinking in front of a huge log fire. All of a sudden, we heard a great whooping noise, accompanied by a terrible roaring. We looked up to see a mob of Blackfeet charging into our camp.

At first, we could not understand where the roaring was coming from. But then we saw that the Blackfeet were driving an enormous grizzly bear straight towards us!

For a few minutes there was total chaos. The Indians ran off screaming with laughter at their great joke and the beast raced about, swiping wildly with its huge claws. My mates all shinned up trees faster than frightened squirrels, and I was left cornered by the grizzly, with nothing but my knife to defend myself.

As the bear lunged at me, it let out a deafening roar. I thrust my hand into its mouth and seized its tongue, using my other hand to plunge my knife into its chest!

A second later a shot rang out and the bear crashed to the earth, a musket ball in its head. One of my companions had saved my life!

So as you can see, life was constantly full of surprises. And, not long after my brush with the grizzly, it took a new, and very unexpected turn indeed.

Bull's Robe Beckwourth

I'd been at the Rendezvous and summer camp of 1828 when an old trapper told me how, just for a joke, he'd told the Crow Indians that I was really one of their own tribe. I'd been kidnapped from them by the Cheyenne years back, then sold to the whites. He said that when he told them, the Crow became very excited and wanted me back. Well, him and me had a good laugh, and then thought no more of it. But that wasn't the end of the matter.

The following winter me and Jim Bridger were out setting traps, when we decided to split up. He took one fork in the river and me the other. We hadn't been parted for long, when I came across a herd of horses grazing

at the riverside. Too late, I realised they were Indian mounts, but by now the two Crows guarding them had pounced on me. They were soon marching me into their village, where I was quickly surrounded by at least a thousand Indians. I now began to feel very scared. Then, to my relief, a whole bunch of Crow came rushing out of their tepee and began hugging and kissing me just like the long-lost relative they believed I was!

And so began that period of my life when I lived as a Crow Indian. In no time I was re-united with my long lost 'sisters' (ha!) Then, not long after that, I met the lovely Pine Leaf. Out of the eight Crow women I loved, there wasn't one to touch her. She was beautiful, brainy and brave and could ride a horse and fight as well as any man.

When she was only twelve, her twin brother had been killed in a raid on our village. She had vowed that she would not marry until she had killed a hundred of the enemy with her own hands. Well, I did ask her to marry me. She said she would, but not until the pine leaves turned yellow. At first this pleased me, but then the thought struck me that pine leaves never do turn yellow, but stay green all year round. I was immediately heart-broken!

But of course, my life with the Crow wasn't all falling in love and getting married. Much of it involved hunting buffalo, stealing horses and battling it out with our tribal enemies. Often I would go out with raiding parties of young braves and attack the Blackfeet, Arapahoes, Cheyenne and Sioux and, as a result of my bravery in these battles, I was soon made a chief. I was known among my Crow brothers as Enemy of the Horses and Bull's Robe.

One battle that sticks in my mind concerns the time we were out hunting buffalo.

We were in a party of about five hundred, led by a chief called Long Haired Chief (on account of his hair, which measured some two and a half metres). We'd been gone from camp about four days, when we came across a large band of Blackfeet. They were well into our territory, but had positioned themselves on a hilltop and were protected all round by huge rocks that made the place a natural fortress.

We sent for reinforcements and two hundred more of our braves arrived. Then all seven hundred of us charged at the Blackfeet, whooping and yelling and firing on them with rifles and bows and arrows.

However, so well were they dug in, that our charges were repeatedly driven back with many of our braves sinking to their knees, pierced by arrows and felled by bullets. It soon began to look like we wouldn't be able to shift them.

Many of our number, including Long Haired Chief, wanted to abandon our attack, but by now my blood was up. I leapt onto a rock and cried to the Crow, "We can kill all of these Blackfeet! But if we run, we will be shot in the back. The Great Spirit has sent these enemies here for us to kill! If we don't, he'll drive away our buffalo and destroy our grasslands. No! We must fight. Follow me and I'll show you how the braves of the white chief fight!"

And with that, not fearing for my safety, I leapt from the rock and ran towards the Blackfeet, looking neither to my right nor left. As I did, I heard a ferocious screaming and shouting from behind me and I knew that the Crow were following, urged on by my mighty speech. Soon we were scrambling up the rocks that surrounded the Blackfeet and engaging them in ferocious hand-to-hand fighting.

I instantly was set upon by two Blackfeet. One of them clung to my back while the other jabbed at me with his hunting knife as

I staggered this way and that to avoid his thrusts. Reaching up, I seized the one on my back and, pulling him over my shoulders, held him above my head, whirled around a few times, then flung him on top of his pal. Then, before either of them could recover, I pulled out my pistol and blasted them both lifeless.

I now looked around me and saw that all over the hilltop my fellow Crow had gained the upper hand in our battle against the Blackfeet and soon the enemy were surrendering in their hundreds.

Reader, I will not continue, for what happened next is just too awful to tell. However, in another twenty minutes or so, every single one of the Blackfeet lay dead.

After this battle, I was disturbed by the Crow's savage behaviour and decided that I would leave them. But as it turned out, I had now become a hero and whenever they were threatened by enemies the Crow would come to me. This made it difficult for me to go.

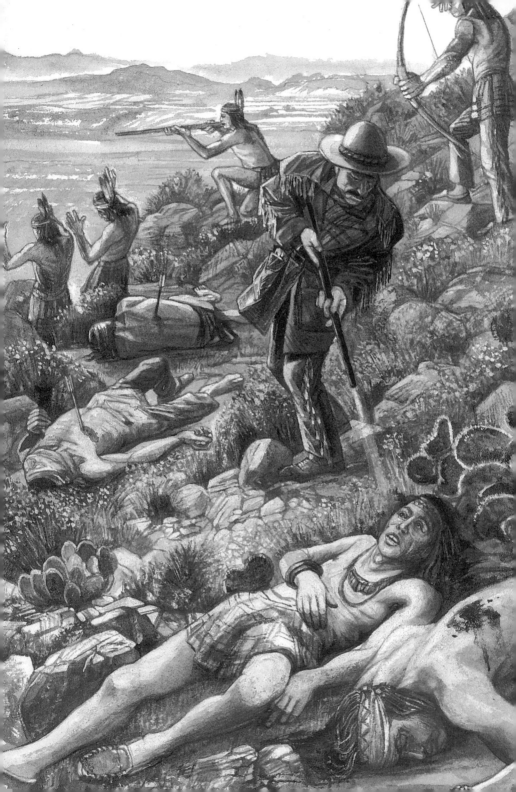

Of course, it suited me in some ways, as I was now well placed to carry out profitable trade with the Crow. They needed guns and **ammo** and the fur companies needed elk skin, beaver pelt and buffalo robes. And I was able to arrange these exchanges.

So I continued my life with the Crow, learning their language and all of their ways. And those of other tribes too. Then, after six years or so of me asking her to be my bride, Pine Leaf finally said "yes" and we were married.

Five weeks after this I left the Crow for good and returned to St Louis. You may say this was a strange thing to do, but I am a restless man, always in search of new things to conquer. I think that, maybe, it was the challenge of making Pine Leaf my wife that had kept me with the Crow so long. Or maybe not? But anyway, I was definitely ready for new adventures.

CHAPTER 4

Swamp Warfare

View of St Louis in 1836

When I entered St Louis in 1836, I hardly recognised it. Just a few years before, when I had worked there with the blacksmith, it had been a cluster of shacks and muddy tracks. Now it had paved streets, shops, warehouses, a theatre and magnificent mansions where rich men lived. But this was the way with so many cities in our fast-growing nation. They sprang up overnight!

As I walked about, I kept my eyes peeled for trouble. Friends had warned me that large sums of money had been offered for my life as it was thought I had been involved in a Crow robbery of some white men.

After some time, I decided to visit the new theatre and during the interval I went into the bar for refreshments. As I did, five dangerous-looking characters advanced on me. One of them said, 'There's the Crow!' and they drew their knives. I, too, pulled my knife from my belt in readiness for a fight. I was just in the middle of uttering a blood-curdling Crow war-whoop prior to hurling myself on my enemies, when the local sheriff walked into the bar. He ordered me to be quiet and although I was boiling with rage, I did as he said. Moments later, my attackers walked off. I tried to follow them – but the sheriff threatened to throw me in gaol so I left.

I now knew I had many enemies. This was confirmed when I heard a terrible rumour that was going around. It was being said that

I was responsible for a plague of smallpox that was now sweeping through the Crow nation and killing many thousands of my old friends. This lie hurt me very deeply.

By the autumn of that same year, I was already tiring of town life and anxious to be off to the wilds again. But the fur trade wasn't what it used to be. Jobs were few and far between. So when a pal told me scouts

were being recruited for a campaign against the Seminole Indians down in the Florida Everglade swamps, I pricked up my ears, especially when I learned what a warm and pleasant place Florida was. And, hoping to find fame and fortune, I travelled to New Orleans, where I joined up as a scout and express rider.

Seminole means wild wanderer and these Indians had fled to the swamps of Florida to escape the westward spread of the white settlers. They weren't the only fugitives in the Everglades. Black slaves who'd run away from the plantations also hid out in the swamps and some of them married Seminoles. But the planters wanted their slaves back and the government wanted the swamps, so General Zachary Taylor organised a force of eight hundred men to drive the Seminoles out.

On October 26 at New Orleans we boarded small boats with our horses but, not being used to sea travel, we didn't secure them with ropes. This was a mistake we would soon regret. We hadn't been at sea long when terrible storms began to toss our boats like matchwood, throwing the poor, terrified horses every-which-way, killing some, and breaking others' legs.

Then, as if this wasn't bad enough, my boat became stuck on a reef. We were stranded for twelve days. Yet more of our horses died of hunger and had to be thrown overboard.

We finally made it to the steamy swamps
and on Christmas Day morning our camp
was surrounded by a force of some four
hundred Indians and black slaves. The Battle
of Okeechobee began!

The enemy were cunning. They hid up
moss-covered trees and popped up all over
the place. They fired their rifles, then dashed
off through the swamps, leaving us all open-
mouthed in amazement. They miraculously
appeared to run across the surface of the
water!

Of course, as we soon discovered, they hadn't run across the swamp at all. They had simply jumped from one underwater hillock to another. Not knowing where these hillocks were, we daren't follow. We feared we might drown or be attacked by the giant alligators and water snakes that lurked everywhere.

Eventually, the Indians and slaves slipped away into the woods leaving over a hundred of our men killed or wounded. But, despite the fact that only eleven Indians were killed, our leaders decided we had achieved a great triumph. I had to ride from one fort to another crying, "Victory!" at each – although I knew it was a lie.

After the battle, I stayed on in Florida for another ten months, scouting and carrying messages. But then I got bored and longed to be off horse-thieving. The Seminoles had no horses worth stealing, so I decided once more to return to St Louis and get myself a fresh job.

CHAPTER

Sante Fe to California

I'd only been in St Louis for five days, when I was hired by Louis Vasquez. He wanted to trade with the Indians of the southern plains. Another chance for excitement! I would be dealing with Cheyennes, Arapahoes and Sioux, all enemies of my old tribe, the Crow.

We set out on the Santa Fe Trail and, when we reached the trading post, Louis made me agent-in-charge. But now I had to find some Indians to trade with. I left the fort and after riding hard, I climbed a small mountain and spotted distant buffalo running in small groups. From this I knew that they'd recently been chased by Indians, so I decided to stay put.

When darkness came, I saw camp fires flickering and I knew I'd found the Cheyenne. In the morning I went to them and said, "I have killed a great Crow Chief and must run away, or be killed by them. I have come to you, the bravest people on the plains, as I do not wish to be killed by any lesser tribe. I have come here to be cut up and thrown out for your dogs to eat."

And then I offered them two ten-gallon kegs of whiskey. And instead of killing me, they began to trade furs. I was in business! The friendship that I began with the Cheyenne that day would last for many years, until the terrible event which I'll tell of later.

My stay at the trading post didn't last long, but during the next few years I continued trading and moving around the south-west until I ended up in Mexico. And it was while I was here in 1846 that war broke out between Mexico and America. My five companions and I were now in the wrong place at the wrong time. But we thought we would make the most of this and we set about stealing horses from Mexican ranches.

Quite soon, we'd collected a tidy little herd of about two thousand animals, which we then began to drive back to America. Of course, the Mexicans didn't take kindly to having their horses stolen and they began to chase after us, firing their guns and yelling like madmen.

It was a thrilling chase, which lasted some four days. As all these hundreds of horses thundered across the plains and splashed through rivers, we occasionally caught sight of our pursuers and saw puffs of rifle smoke, then felt their bullets go whistling past our ears. But we had one advantage! Our

A band of horse-thieves returning from a
raid into Mexico

pursuers were mounted on one horse each. But we had hundreds! Whenever our horse tired, we'd simply leap, mid-gallop, from its back to that of the nearest mustang. This way we eventually lost the Mexicans.

Back in America, I took a job carrying messages and acting as a guide and interpreter for the army. I also bought a hotel in Santa Fe, which my partner looked after while I carried out my army duties. The war continued for two more years until America won, and took over all of northern Mexico which then included California.

I continued to work as a despatch rider, often crossing dangerous Indian territory and during my journeys I was frequently chased by hostile tribes. On one occasion, I was trapped between two large war parties of Pawnees. To add to my troubles, my horse was worn out, so I had no choice but to dig myself into the ground.

I hunkered down in my hidey-hole like a scared jackrabbit and pulled some big rocks on top of myself. Minutes later, I listened to the Pawnees galloping this way and that as they searched for me. One of them almost rode his pony on top of my head! My heart thumping like a war-drum, I stayed curled in my burrow until I was sure it was safe to come out. Then I stole a fresh horse and continued my journey.

In 1848 my feet became itchy, so I travelled to California where I became a despatch rider once again. It was while I was delivering the post in this new job that I witnessed a most terrible tragedy, the awful memory of which remains with me still.

On my various journeys delivering mail, I often rested at the Christian Mission of St Miguel. I liked this place because it was run by Mr Reed, an Englishman, and he and his family were most pleasant company. On this occasion I arrived at dusk and as usual I walked in, but was surprised that no one was around.

I then went into the kitchen and saw someone on the floor fast asleep, or so I thought. I pushed the man with my foot, but he didn't wake or move. It was then that I realised that something was very wrong.

I quickly went to my horse and got my pistols, then returned to the kitchen. Lighting a candle, I began to search the house. In the corridor, I stumbled over something slumped on the floor. I held my candle out and with horror saw that it was the body of a woman!

I now entered a room and there I found yet another body, which I recognised as that of the Reed's Indian maid.

I was about to enter the next room, but as my hand reached for the doorknob a warning voice in my head told me to stop.

Feeling really scared, I quickly left, found my horse and galloped ninety miles to the nearest town for help. I returned to the Mission some time later with a **posse**. On entering the house, we found no less than eleven murdered people!

They included Mr Reed and his wife and children! Quite near to them someone had tried to start a fire, obviously intending to burn the Mission and them in it.

Some time after this, four wicked white men were arrested and found guilty of the murders. They had been guests of the Reeds, who had kindly given them beds and food. And I had been right not to open that door. The murderers later confessed that they were on the other side of it, their pistols cocked ready to blast me to eternity should I attempt to enter their hiding place!

I decided to try my luck elsewhere.

The year before a man called John Sutter had spotted a chunk of gold in his millstream and thousands of men were now racing to California, hoping to strike it rich. Many had, too! Some even by accident.

One man was sitting on a rock feeling homesick and dispirited because he hadn't found gold, so he got up and kicked the rock. The rock rolled aside and underneath there was an enormous nugget!

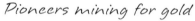
Pioneers mining for gold

Prospector panning for gold.
Photo taken in 1890

Another bunch of prospectors were burying their dead friend and while the preacher droned on they began fidgeting with the dirt from the grave. The next moment one yelled "Gold!" Yes, it was in the grave! The preacher abandoned the sermon and everyone leapt in and started digging.

So I thought it was time I looked at California's goldfields!

6

My Beautiful Valley

Men were striking it rich in the hills of
California, but I didn't want to spend my
days crouched over freezing streams panning
for gold. Instead, I moved from one frontier
town to the next, playing the card game they
call monte.

I'm a keen gambler and some nights I won
thousands of dollars. But, money is of no
great importance to me. I spent my winnings
buying drinks for every man in town, and
soon they were too drunk to stand up! Any I
had left, I gave to the poor.

In 1850, I tired of gambling. I headed into
a wild and lonely region of the Sierra Nevada
Mountains with some friends and, while they
panned for gold, I went off hunting.

It was while I was tracking a deer that I

noticed a distant mountain pass that seemed much lower than all the others. I suspected that this might lead right through from the Sierras to California.

At this time in America's history, thousands of people from the east were trying to make their way west to a new life in California, which many saw as paradise on earth. However, in order to do this they first had to cross the Sierra Nevada Mountains. This was a most difficult journey made doubly dangerous by hostile Indians, freezing blizzards, grizzlies and wolves.

In 1846 a wagon train of about ninety people had become snowed up in the Sierras. Half had frozen to death and the survivors were forced to eat not only their own pets, but also their dead companions! A new and quicker route through the Sierras would mean that wagon trains would be much safer. With this in mind my companions and I decided to explore that distant pass.

After many days trekking across snow-covered peaks, we entered an enormous grassy valley full of wild flowers and beautiful birds. Flocks of ducks and geese sailed over our heads or swam on the crystal clear waters of the river, which meandered along the valley. None of the creatures were in the slightest bit afraid of us.

It was then that I knew that no man, save for a few Indians, had ever entered this valley before. I also knew that it would make an ideal wagon route into California.

My friends and I now set about making a road through the valley and in July 1851

I proudly led my first wagon train of settlers through my pass to California. Quite soon, long lines of covered wagons were making their way through the mountains and into that beautiful valley.

In 1852 I built myself a trading post in this lovely spot. Now the tired and hungry settlers would have somewhere to rest and stock up on supplies before the last leg of their journey into sunny California. My new home was in the most perfect place on earth; the scenery was breathtaking, the grass lush, the water plentiful and risk of attack by Indians slim.

I soon had fields full of vegetables growing around my little homestead, flocks of sheep grazing the meadows and a hundred or so fine ponies. I was constantly busy with the wagon trains which never failed to stop. I sold them food and supplies, repaired their **Prairie Schooners** and generally gave them advice and encouragement.

And then, as has always been the case in my life, after seven years of being snug and happy in my beautiful valley, things changed. I'd been having a few problems. People had been failing to pay for my services and there had been rumours flying around about me and stolen ponies. Also around this time, I organised a foot race between a black boy and an Indian boy. And on a wild impulse, I bet everything I owned on the black boy to win.

Knowing the Indian was a good runner and not wanting to lose everything, I took the precaution of finding another black boy, about the same size and appearance as the

first. I had him hide behind a tree, about half way around the one mile race course. Then, when the first boy reached him he nipped out from the tree and put on a tremendous spurt.

But luck wasn't with me that day. Despite being fresh, he still didn't catch up with the Indian boy who ran like the wind so I ended

up losing almost everything. Well, I shrugged off my bad luck. Then, deciding that I was getting too old for mountain winters anyway, I saddled up my remaining horse and journeyed back east, calling on old Indian pals as I did so.

My Betrayal of Friends

After many scrapes and adventures, I eventually fetched up in Denver City where I opened up a store and saloon. Well, as has happened so often, trouble soon found me out in my new life of storekeeper and saloon owner.

One day, I was laid up in bed with a fever when a ferocious giant of a man called Bill Payne came to my saloon looking for a fight. While talking to my barmaid he suddenly tried to pull her ring from her finger. Hearing her screams, I rushed downstairs and told Payne to leave but he refused. Then we both saw a double-barrelled shotgun in one corner of the room, grabbed it and began to struggle.

At this moment, two of my customers came to my rescue and helped me throw Payne out of the saloon. Payne was back in minutes though and, as he rushed at me, I seized the gun and shot him.

Roaring with pain and anger he now crashed from room to room before falling into the fireplace and dying. Half an hour later, I was charged with Payne's murder and locked in the town gaol. My trial followed soon afterwards and when it was time for the jury to give their verdict, every one of them said, "Not guilty!" Some even told me later I'd done a good job, getting rid of one of Denver's worst trouble makers.

Not longer after my trial, the citizens of Denver were in a state of panic following Indian attacks on the outlying settlements. Colonel John Chivington decided that the way to solve the problem was to wipe out all the Indians in the area and formed a regiment of some seven hundred and fifty men to do just that.

Because of my expert knowledge of the Cheyenne I was approached to act as their guide. I didn't want to, as I knew the local Cheyenne were a peaceful bunch but Chivington was out for blood. Fearing he'd hang me if I refused, I did as he asked and led him and his men to Sand Creek, the place where I knew the Indians were.

When we finally reached the ridge overlooking the camp, we saw the tepees of Chief Black Kettle and his people spread along the riverbank below us. I knew that all those Indians were innocent and completely unprepared for an attack, believing they were protected by a peace treaty.

Colonel Chivington then gave orders to begin the killing and his men charged down on the unsuspecting Cheyenne, shooting as they went. From my spot on the ridge I saw an old friend, Spotted Antelope, come running of his tepee, shouting, "Stop! Stop!" but they shot him along with six or seven children who were playing at the river's edge and a bunch of women standing by the cooking pots.

During the next three hours hundreds of innocent Indians aged from one week to eighty years were killed by the whites, who only lost nine men. And then the victorious soldiers paraded through the streets of Denver, while crowds cheered them to the skies. To think I was part of that terrible day fills me with shame that will stay with me forever.

After the massacre the Indians went on the warpath. Because of my terrible betrayal, my own conscience wouldn't let me alone and early last year, I set out to find the camp of the Cheyenne.

After some days I came upon their tepees and entered the lodge of Leg-In-The-Water. To my shame, he asked if I'd brought more white men to finish killing Indian families. So I told him I'd come to ask the Indians to make peace with the whites because there were now just too many for them to fight.

But then he told me the Indians didn't care if they died fighting the whites, because they'd taken and killed everything they loved:

their prairies, forests, rivers, horses, buffalo... and now their families.

And I understand what he meant. As the settlers move ever westwards, I, too, am seeing the wild open spaces and wonders of nature I love so dearly all disappearing as they build ever more towns and cities.

It's 1866 now and I'm an old man. In my lifetime I've seen much of America change from wilderness to civilisation and I often wonder what this country will look like in a hundred and fifty years' time. Will the

great herds of bison and deer still roam the prairies? Will bands of braves still gallop across the plains yelling with the sheer joy of being alive in this magnificent country which the Great Spirit created?

All this talk of Indians has got me thinking of my old friends, the Crow, so I'll stop writing now and pay them a visit. It's been good putting all this down for you. I hope you've enjoyed reading it as much as I've enjoyed writing it.

James Pierson Beckwourth

Story Background

October 1866

Epilogue

Jim Beckwourth did go to see the Crow and whilst with them, he died. There are various stories about how this happened. Some say he simply got a nosebleed, then passed away. Others say that he went hunting bison. His horse threw him and he was trampled to death. And some say the Crow poisoned him, so his spirit would stay with them forever. But however he died, spending his last hours amongst the Indians seemed a very fitting end to his amazing life.

Some of the resources I used as research for this story are as follows: On microfiche: Published by Harper and Bros (1856), The Life and Adventures of James P Beckwourth, as told to Thomas D Bonner – various reprints have followed. Jim Beckwourth by Elinor Wilson (1972), University of Oklahoma Press.

There's also his official website http://www.beckwourth.org/ Many of the US websites emphasise that he was a great African-American, probably as a justifiable reaction to the 1952 film in which he was portrayed by a white actor .

Index

• •

Glossary

Ammo (abbreviation) ammunition

Critter a creature

Independence a Declaration of Independence was signed on 4 July 1776

Pardners partners, comrades

Posse a body of people summoned by a sheriff for peacekeeping

Prairie Schooners a covered wagon used by the 19th century pioneers in crossing the North American prairies

Skedaddle to run away

Squitty anything of significance